My Garden
My Homeplace

Ann Ballard

My Garden My Homeplace

ISBN-10: 1500188980

Dedication

In memory of my parents,
whose daughter I was always proud to be.

Acknowledgments

I am grateful to the following people
for their help in making this book:
Caroline Pugh, Suzie Daugherty,
Shelbbie Daugherty, David Smothers, Dedra Thomas,
Kristie Lauderdale, Chris Hysaw and Adam Armour

.

My Garden My Homeplace

Chapter One

Eponymous communities are scattered about the state of Mississippi. I grew up in Ballardsville.

From *Biographical and Historical Memoirs of Mississippi* embracing an authentic and comprehensive account of the chief events in the history of the State, and a record of the lives of many of the most worthy and illustrious families and individuals. Published in 1891.

John A. Ballard, a farmer and merchant of Ballardsville, Itawamba County, Miss., was born in South Carolina, April 14, 1827, a son of Thomas C. and Rebecca (Grimes) Ballard, both of whom were natives of Virginia. The mother was a member of the Baptist Church and the father in every way favored and supported it. They had five children born to them: Andrew J., Thomas C., William, Susan, and John A., above mentioned, who is the only one in the family now living, and who was the second in order of birth. He came to Mississippi when young, and located in Itawamba County. His education was begun in South Carolina, and was finished here in the common schools. January 3, 1849, he married Jane E. Sandlin, who was born April 7, 1827, in South Carolina, a daughter of James and Elizabeth (Gregory) Sandlin, and the third in their family of ten children: Mary, Alfred, Jackson, Jessie (deceased), Green (deceased), Thomas (deceased), Sarah (deceased), John R. (deceased), Sisley (deceased) and Jane E.

To Mr. and Mrs. Ballard were born fourteen children: Thomas C. married Sallie E. Cooper; Andrew J. married Anna Cason; William D. married Ida Bowlin; James M. married Ida Jones; David S. married Trannie Keyes; George W. married Ada Francis; Finis E. married Della Lanford; Joseph B, Elijah F., Rebecca became the wife of W.F. Watson; Mary married W. A. Williams; Marcia V. married J. H. Pearce; Eva J., John A. Jr. (deceased), married Maggie Francis. Mr. Ballard enlisted in 1862, in Captain Boulden's company

1

and served in a Mississippi regiment under General Goulston for a time, later serving under Major Ham in the campaign through northern Mississippi. Later in 1863 he hired a substitute and returned home. Afterward, when the law was passed prohibiting the employment of substitutes, he again took the field in the fall of 1864, and served under General Goulston in General Forrest's command until the close of the war. He and his wife are members of the Missionary Baptist Church, and his children are either members or attendants of the same. Politically he is a democrat. He has lived on his present plantation since 1850, and may be fairly regarded as one of the pioneers of the county. He began merchandising in 1871, and carried a large stock of goods adapted to the needs of the community, having the only store at Ballardsville. He is the owner of about twenty-five hundred acres of land and has on his place a steam cotton gin and sawmill. These statements may be taken as some indication of the fact that he ranks among the wealthy men of the county, and it may be also added to his credit that he has been the architect of his own fortune, his large possessions having been gained through his own unaided efforts. While he has been accumulating for himself, he has not been unmindful of the needs of others, and has ever been liberal in his contributions to all causes tending to the general good. He is a Master Mason.

I spent many years feeling embarrassed when asked where I was from. There was absolutely nothing to reply other than Ballardsville. I didn't name it. I still feel a twinge when I say it and I hope people don't think I'm being pretentious, or worse, lying.

I fled the family farm in 1961 when I went off to Ole Miss to get a Bachelor of Music degree. In 1983 I returned to the farm and restored my great-grandfather's house, which was built in 1883.

One hundred years after it was built, I moved into it. I love it a lot. Every time I have maintenance work done, the workmen brag on how well and sturdily it is built. My heart fairly bursts with pride.

There was a dog trot with two fifteen ft. x fifteen ft. rooms on either side, both with a chimney on the outside wall. The remaining four rooms – dining, kitchen, two bedrooms – were built behind these two rooms. The ceilings are almost nine feet high and the baseboards are twelve inches tall. I believe this was a generic house plan because five or so miles down the road there is a house with the same plan. It hasn't been kept up and is in a state of collapse. When bathrooms came along, one was built on the back porch causing one to have to leave the house to use it. That was rectified with my restoration.

The dog trot was enclosed before I can recall and now holds my library. I am absolutely a bibliophile, reading fiction from the public library and collecting art and gardening books. I have always loved books, the look of them, the feel of them, and sometimes, the way they smell. I remember loving the smell of the bookmobile when I was a child. Books transport and edify me. I have finished more than one novel and wondered, Why isn't this author in charge of the planet?

Some years ago I was called by a telemarketer and the conversation went like this:

Telemarketer: Do you own your own home?

Me: Sure do.

Telemarketer: Does the exterior have to be painted?

Me: Sure does.

Telemarketer: Have you ever thought about aluminum siding?

Me: Sure have.

Telemarketer: Would you like us to come and give you an estimate?

Me: Sure wouldn't.

Telemarketer: Well! You can't say anything without sure, sure, sure.

She slammed the phone down right in my ear. Victory on my side wouldn't you say?

Before electricity came to Ballardsville the house was lit by carbide which was also piped down to my grandparents' house. The tank is still in my yard. There was a well house, a smoke house, a cook's house, a storm house, and a mule barn across the road. The yard slopes down to a pond from which the mules drank. The occasional fisherman still tries his luck at this pond today. The people drank water from the well and it provided water to be boiled in a wash-pot with a fire built under it for doing laundry.

After a few years the white paint on the exterior of my house began to bore and pall. I had it painted pink, influenced by seventeen years of living in the decidedly un-boring French Quarter in New Orleans, a place I continue to love. The present-day Quarter is much changed from the neighborhood it was when I lived there. I count it a genuine privilege to have lived there when I did. People who are unfamiliar with the Quarter perceive it as a dangerous den of iniquity. The residents go about their daily lives the same as the people in the suburbs. Well, they're probably a mite more interesting. The police are everywhere and there's daily garbage collection. Gotta keep it safe and nice for the tourists, who flock to Bourbon Street, a place largely ignored by the residents.

I lived in five different apartments and, happily, four of them had balconies where I could grow plants which I was drawn to since childhood. My father farmed and my mother always had a large vegetable garden and the usual ornamental shrubs and flowers. Gardening was, and is, in my blood.

Need I mention how culturally shocking it was to relocate from the laissez-faire climate of the French Quarter to the strongly un-laissez-faire climate of the Bible Belt that grips northeast Mississippi? Nevertheless, I made it and I've given the background before coming to my garden of three or four acres where I have gardened all these years to make something beautiful to me. It is my creation, and mine alone.

The cook's house can be seen in this photo behind my first cousin, Barbara Sheffield Ewer, about age twelve. It was last lived in by a bachelor named Kelbus Gasaway. Mr. Kelbus cleaned the graveyards. He and his sister, Gertrude Tackett, occasionally filled in at Ballardsville Baptist Church with Mr. Kelbus leading the singing while Miss Gertude hammered away at the piano, sans pedal. After Mr. Kelbus died, the cook's house was taken down.

House with addition, 1946

My House today

Old Pond

In 1983 there were trees: a sweetgum, a mulberry, a black walnut, two shag-bark hickories bearing "hicker-nuts" as we called them, three oaks, two pecans, and a pink crape myrtle artfully planted in the center of the yard. I feel sure the nut and berry-bearing trees were planted to provide food when the house was built. They are majestic today. One of the pecans has an elm growing in its crotch.

The sweetgum balls and black walnuts are problematic in the spring when it's time to mow. I can't bear the sound of them damaging my lawn mower blade. The black walnuts are easily picked up by my nut-grabber. The sweetgum balls number in the thousands and I have spent a lot of money having them raked. If left where they fall, they clog and stop the lawn mower blades. I've considered getting a couple of over-sized people to walk on them and press them into the ground. I think it's a pretty good idea and I haven't discarded it.

In 1984, my parents and I planted a row of eleven white crape myrtles on the south edge of the yard beside the road. We moved them from an old house place. Therefore, they are not hybrids and bloom only once in July. I don't perform crape murder on them so they are tall and lean together over the road where they drop their white flowers. I prefer them to the ever-blooming hybrids and I like that they are from some planted by a gardener many years ago. They suit my house.

Here's what my gardening experience has taught me. I get a tetanus shot every ten years. Here's how Webster's New World Dictionary of the American Language defines tetanus: "an acute infectious disease, often fatal, caused by the specific toxin of a bacillus which usually enters the body through wounds: it is characterized by spasmodic contractions and rigidity of some or all of the voluntary muscles, esp. of the jaw, face, and neck; lockjaw." Wouldn't that put a hitch in my get-along? I always wear gloves. There are gardeners who like to feel the soil with their bare hands and I wish them luck.

Lots of "stuff" has been discarded during the years my house was inhabited. Remember, there was no garbage pick-up in those days. When I dig I frequently find shards of glass, pottery, wire and bricks. I have unearthed a child's shoe and an adult's shoe-heel. And someone had a serious snuff addiction. I have innumerable little brown snuff bottles, some of which I use as vases. If I'm lucky I find an intact handmade brick paver, larger than most and with finger prints on it.

I have gardening attire: underpinnings, long trousers, long-sleeved shirts, protective shoes and socks, sunglasses and a hat. And underneath it all, sunscreen, sunscreen, sunscreen. Dirt and sweat do a number on everything I wear but not on my person.

Eleven white crape myrtles

**March 8, 2008
Snow from the night
President Bill Clinton came to Tupelo.**

My mother was born in 1915, and she knew the sun was her skin's enemy. She never even went to the mailbox without wearing a hat. When Mother went wild berry picking, she swathed herself in one of Daddy's long-sleeved khaki shirts and a pair of his khaki pants with the ankles tied. That extra effort was to protect against the chigger. The minute she got home, it was into the bathtub for a good scrub in case a wiley chigger had made it past her barriers.

She set the example for protecting her skin and I follow it. A complimentary remark was from a stranger to whom I explained the wearing of my hat by saying, "It's for protection from the sun because I spend a large part of the day outside." "You don't look like you've ever been outside", she responded. My mother would have been happy.

When I was a child everybody had a chinaberry tree in their yard. They were exquisite in form and flower. After the flowers came the berries, the perfect size for stuffing up into the nostril of a child my size. Which I did. Unlike my mother, I was calm about the episode, knowing Mother would make everything all right. Which she did. I wish I could recall how she extricated the thing but too many years have passed.

I would have hated to have been my mother. I lived a life of terror: of the world coming to an end and my going to hell, of being kidnapped - I was a neurotic mess. Also, I was about the size of a mosquito and prone to fainting dead away. Of course I was taken to a doctor, and my great-uncle Burr Riley, who was a pharmacist, gave me every new vitamin that came out. Nothing helped. I was an insomniac and a bed-wetter into the elementary school years. Mother, bless her, never chastised me as she got up night after night to change the wet sheets to dry ones. I digress.

I made friends with gardeners. They gave me wise advice and shared plants with me. So many of my prizes have come from the gardens of friends. The come-back begonia, for example. Not a perennial begonia, or a self-seeding begonia, but a come-back begonia. The first one I was given didn't fare well so I relegated it to the compost heap. The next summer I saw a lovely, healthy plant flourishing in the heap. I potted it up and the friend who gave it to me said, "Why, that's a come-back begonia!" Yes, it was. I usually have good luck with begonias but the come-back flummoxes me. I am now on my fourth one and remain hopeful.

Come-back begonia

I was advised by multiple books and magazines to have my soil tested and I heeded this advice. The tests not only told me what my soil needed but when to apply it! How wonderful is that!

A rain gauge is essential to my watering routine and for my record keeping, which I do in two journals. A weather vane and a bat house are part of my arsenal, also. I installed the bat house in 2011, and so far I've had no bats. I'm hoping this year, 2014, will be the one.

Chapter Three

The flowers whose passing I mourn the most are the daffodils/narcissus. They just do not hang around long enough for me. I actually cry, "Don't go, please don't go."

Ice Follies are the first to bloom, usually in mid-February. The ones I ordered multiplied mightily, and I think everybody should have a planting of them whether they know it or not. I am of the opinion that their spirit would be nourished, even if sub-consciously. In the beginning, the flowers have a yellow, ruffled center surrounded by lighter yellow petals. Later they fade to almost white. They are borne on tall, strong stems and are perfect for bringing inside. In fact, they are my favorite flowers for bringing inside because they don't drop their petals and make a mess as many other flowers do.

It was with dismay that I heard that some daffodils don't bloom forever. My absolute favorites which I bought pre-1992 journal keeping, so I don't know their name, have bloomed scantily the last two years. I thought maybe they had gotten too deep or too crowded and I plan to get my shovel and investigate. I bet I'm right and I'll have them flowering again.

I have an enormous variety. I have King Alfred which, I'm

18

told, is no longer available. Happily, there is a hybrid that mimics King Alfred and is superior in both size and color. It's amazingly beautiful. There's nothing like a cobalt blue vase full of yellow daffodils, if you ask me.

Because they do multiply so freely, they're great for swapping. I like to order several new kinds every year and split the cost and quantity with a friend. Otherwise I will end up with a daunting number of bulbs to plant and a higher cost to pay.

There are three kinds that were here when I moved in, in addition to a swath of naturalized paperwhite narcissus. I don't cut the foliage of any of them until the last week in June. If I want flowers the next year, that's what I have to do. It's a good thing I'm not a stickler for a perfect yard.

I don't have a lawn, I have a yard. My only nice grass is St. Augustine in the square garden and centipede in the west field. The rest of my big, sprawley yard has awful stuff growing on it. I'm just happy it's green stuff. My two wonderful mutts, Coco and Chuck E., whom I plucked from the side and middle of the road, respectively, love to scratch for cool dirt to lie in during the hot summer. I don't mind, they harm nothing important.

I have ignored tulips since I learned they don't re-bloom.

Chapter Four

After reading gardening magazines and books about gardening, I was inspired to make a square garden. It is 23 feet x 23 feet and has a 40-inch entrance and a 40-inch exit, wide enough to push a wheelbarrow through. I have three wheelbarrows, and they're all busy constantly. This garden was to be my Sistine Chapel, exquisitely planted, immaculately groomed and formal.

A formal garden is one that is planted symmetrically: if the plan were folded down the middle, the two sides would be identical. I laid St. Augustine grass and placed a square birdbath in the center. I planted the bones of it. The following plants, two of each, make up the garden's bones:

- aster, Stokesia
- amsonia
- aucuba
- baptisia, Prairie Blue Eyes
- canna, black, in tall urns at the back exit
- deutzia, dwarf white
- fatsia

- four o'clocks, yellow, from seed collected outside Liuzza's Restaurant in New Orleans, pre-Katrina

- hydrangeas, Annabelle, Incrediball

- Indian Pink, native

- ivy, variegated, supported by two handsome metal forms

- maiden grass

- roses, yellow pass-alongs, pink pass-alongs

- salvia, Indigo Spires

- spirea, Anthony Waterer

There are two bluepoint junipers at the front outside corners, and two red Formosa azaleas at the back outside corners. There are four concrete urns at the inside corners planted with whatever strikes my fancy. I won't name all my choices, but I will say, as a plant collector, I don't show a lot of restraint.

A wooden pergola was built over the back exit to accommodate coral honeysuckle in the spring and summer and sweet autumn clematis in the fall. Some years into its existence I laid a border of old pavers, inside and out, to form a much-needed boundary between the garden and the yard.

Come spring, I plant annuals, both seed and plantlets, for summer bloom. "Voluptuous" was the word I had in mind this year when I planted zinnias, Siam Queen Basil, and vinca plantlets of every hue. I love vinca – the colors, the way they make a bushy plant, the way they re-seed themselves if one is patient, and the way they bloom until the first freeze gets them.

Other plants, perennial or self-seeding, scattered throughout the garden are:

- alliums
- balsam
- baptisia, white
- campion, alba
- columbines My favorite is a native that produces masses of delicate, soft red flowers. It re-seeds itself wantonly. It was a pass-along.
- daisies, Clara Curtis and others
- daylilies
- gardenia
- gooseneck loosestrife
- hellebores
- iris
- lilies, Blackberry, Formosa, Oriental, crinum alba
- Opar's Jewels
- phlox, native and hybrid
- platycodin, pink, blue
- salvia, many varieties

I don't have an iris bed or a daylily bed. I mix them among the rest of the plants , so when their blooms fade they are not noticed as an expanse of plants that have gone by.

In mid-July, the Formosa lilies start leaning over with the weight of their big, white buds. I started with one gathered from an old house place. Since that one, they have re-seeded themselves with abandon. They're in the square garden higgeldy-piggeldy and in the yard surrounding it. Some are eight feet tall and have come up through a double-pink althea and a bluepoint juniper. They are luminous in the crepuscular hours.

The square garden contains only white, pale yellow, pink, lavender and blue colors. Is it immaculately groomed? Alas, nothing in my big, sprawley, three-acres-plus-grounds is immaculately groomed.

Square Garden

Square Garden in Autumn

Back corner of Square Garden

Chapter Five

If the square garden was planted with white, pastel, and gray shades, what was I to do with the red, orange, and bright yellow specimens? I had to dig a mixed border where I would plant everything hot and garish. Digging is my specialty - I adore it. The border is fifteen ft. x forty ft. Then, realizing it needed boundaries, I had a white lattice fence with pink posts to match my house erected at the border's back. The front is defined by a lovely border of dark brown pavers with graceful curves at either end. Planted along the fence are a yellow Lady Banksia rose and sweet autumn clematis, which is aggressive to the extreme. I cope with it by running the lawn mower over it.

I have four mowers: a single-blade Airens that I ride, a double-blade Murray that I ride, a gasoline-powered mower that I push, and a reel mower that I push. Among them they meet my every need whether it be expanses or close quarters.

I do everything in my garden except get up high and use a chain saw. I have both a gas-powered weed eater and an electric weed eater but my aversion to them prevents my using them. I really wish I could and I've tried more than once, but I hate them. I rejoice in the fact that I'm healthy enough and strong enough to do the work I love.

Daylilies, red-hot poker, yellow and red zinnias, Lady in Red salvia, canna Pretoria, and tithonia, aka Mexican sunflower, bloom here. Spots of white vinca, elephant ears, banana trees and castor bean play their part. I must say it is eye-poppingly brilliant!

Mixed Border

Another view of Mixed Border

My conservatory is twelve ft. x twenty ft. and is on the north side of my house. It was added in 1991 and is the best darn-tootin' idea I've ever had. (Not really the best. I'm quoting the man who invented the Moon Pie.) It enhances my house, which is a plain farmhouse. Of course, it's as useful as it is decorative. There are plants here year 'round, more during winter than summer. They're all in pretty pots on pretty stands on pretty tables. A white wicker chaise lounge, a wicker rocker, and an ice cream parlor chair, all with white cushions, provide a perfect place to retreat from mosquitoes and other insects. Yes, there is a ceiling fan. The front porch swing is still my favorite resting place. Usually I have a cat lying on my stomach and a dog or two lying near me.

Surrounding the conservatory is a border of four ft. eight inches wide containing only green or white plants. They are:

- variegated Solomon seal
- arborvitae fern
- holly fern
- white iris

- white daylilies
- lily of the valley
- Japanese anemone Whirlwind
- white platycodin

Directly behind the brick border are a profusion of snowdrops and several kinds of daffodils whose names I do not know because I bought them before 1992, pre-record- keeping days.

There is a fern and hosta area on the north side of my house between the chimney and conservatory, quite shady. I don't put the hostas in the ground because some of my gardening friends have lost theirs to voles or moles and I don't want to risk it. So I pot them on when they need it. During the winter I stash them under the ornamental grasses in the square garden and they survive what Mother Nature sends them.

I've rarely seen a fern I didn't covet. How can they all be so gloriously different? Most of mine are in pots due to their inability to withstand freezing temperatures. They go in the greenhouse usually at the end of October when the tropicals are stored.

I read that truly sophisticated gardeners primarily go for the foliage because it's always there. I count myself among them. Heucheras – I'm always seduced by their foliage but they don't live up to the designation of "perennial." Perhaps our heat melts them.

Conservatory exterior

Conservatory interior

Japanese Anemone Whirlwind

Platycodin with putto

Climbing fern

After I ran out of space to plant things in the square garden, mixed border, and conservatory border, I looked west where there was an expanse of mowed field. Relief! Mother Nature and I abhor a vacuum, or, at least a swath of grass devoid of flora.

Plant collectors are not known for their knowledge of garden design. I fall into that category. I began with pairs of American, Arrowwood, and Burkwood viburnums planted in an attractive pattern that I planned to continue. That did not come to pass due to the quantity and variety of plants that I continued to acquire. Someone asked me once, "What do you have in your garden?" I answered, "Name something. If I don't have it I had it and it died."

Oh, it pains me to write this! There are roses, iris, daylilies, wigelia and on and on. Really on and on with no design in mind. How could there be? I knew I would be adding plants so there was no predicting where they would be planted. I probably should have hired a designer. It's too late now.

This garden is planted in centipede grass which I think is beautifully thick and I know is very hard to mow. It has to be mowed with a push-mower due to being planted so densely. I live in my own wellness center.

Here's a sad tale: In 2010 I ordered a Peony Top 10 Collection. It was fall and the ground was utterly dry due to lack of rain. I doggedly soaked the spots where the peonies were to be planted. This did not happen in a day. Finally I was able to dig holes for them. The following spring three of them bloomed. I know, I know. Peonies need a cold winter and we didn't have one, had not had one in years. There are some things I so desperately desire that I ignore the facts believing I can overcome them. Sometimes, but very seldom, I prevail. This was not one of those times.

I saw a bat plant (tacca) in bloom at the National Botanical Garden and the hair stood up on the back of my neck. I would give my spleen for one! I ordered it three times. The last one was a white one. I also ordered seed. It was not to be.

The last addition to this garden was a seventy-foot long border of hyperion daylilies with various iris planted close behind. The iris will be gone by when the daylilies bloom.

There is an iron arbor, welded by a friend, eight ft. high, nine ft. long, and three ft. wide. Crossvine is planted at its four posts.

A vine I plant every year from ordered seeds is mina lobata. It blooms in the fall. For climbers, I plant landscaping timbers, wrap them in chicken wire for the vines to cling to, and top them with a finial.

This description of the west field garden will come to a close with a list of plants in the garden proper and a list of plants in its proximity:

- abelia Frances Mason
- amsonia
- daylilies
- duranta I lift these and put them in the greenhouse for the winter.
- honeysuckle Peaches and Cream
- iris
- lespedeza, weeping
- peonies
- roses
- spirea, Vanhouttei
- sweetspire,Virgina
- vitex I have two of these, one native and one hybrid. The hybrid is the bluest, bordering on purple. Both are beloved by bees. The common name for the vitex tree is chaste tree, so called, the story goes, because monks chewed the leaves to quell their libido.
- Weigela, named after Christian E. von Weigel, a German botanist. My cultivar is Wine and Roses
- Wisteria, Amethyst Falls and Snow Showers

PROXIMITY:

- althea, double pink
- beauty berry

- camellia, white single

- 2 chestnut trees

- clethra

- fringe tree

- kolkwitzia I spied this shrub in full bloom in a magazine many years ago. I had to have one. This was pre-worldwide web; I can't imagine how I tracked it down. Sometimes I wonder what I could have accomplished if I had applied this tenacity to another field.

- locust Purple Robe

- magnolia, saucer, star. Oddly, I've never even considered planting our state magnolia. I can't say why.

- maple, Japanese 2

- oxydendron, one of my favorites

- pittisporum

- poplar, tulip

- sweet olive One of two varieties in my yard. In my opinion, nothing equals its fragrance.

I want to add to this area a China berry tree and a Chinese Seven-Son-Flower (heptacodium miciniodes).

70' long border of hyperion daylilies, vitex tree, cryptomeria, other daylilies, containers with Meyer lemon, ornamental peach standard, pineapple sage, coleus, dahlias

The picture of me in my garden isn't typical, nor is it recent. But the bloomers are still there. Most of the time I resemble a filthy troglodyte. If the temperature is seventy degrees or higher and I'm standing still watering something, I'm immediately soaked with sweat, starting with my underpinnings. I cling to the belief that all the impurities in my body are leached out through my sweat.

Front Porch

My front porch makes me very happy. It is ten ft. deep and forty ft. long and is on the east side of my house. That means that during the summer it isn't in the sun after lunch. It's perfect for retiring to after an arduous morning of gardening. I peel off my sweat-soaked duds, hang them on the porch furniture to dry, and change to dry duds. I train the floor-stand fan on the swing and I lie down amongst the pillows. I make the swing rock with my toes on the chain from which it is suspended. I read, then sleep a little, read some more, sleep....Ballardsville is still a farming community and I like seeing the tractors go by pulling loads of hay. I'm surrounded by peace.

In addition to the swing whose support hooks were put in the ceiling by my forebears, there's an old set of wooden furniture, a two-seater and two single-seaters, all on rockers. I have a collection of plant stands and tables which are all occupied with plants. Typically, there are about sixty plants on the porch.

There's a wonderful, old iron-cross begonia, a pass-along, that I put in the same stand in the same place on the porch every year. Every year a bird, a wren, I believe, builds a nest in it and lays three eggs. She does not choose wisely. My cat lies in wait for the eggs to hatch, then jumps up into the begonia and it's bye-bye, birdies. Next summer I plan to remove the nest early on, thereby preventing mother bird's and my heartbreak...and considerable damage to the iron-cross begonia which recuperates in my greenhouse over the winter.

There are six wooden posts on the porch with waist-high surrounds that are the perfect size for accommodating plants in various-sized containers. There are always six pots of purple achimines given to me years ago by someone I can no longer recall. I am still really appreciative as they bloom reliably and profusely. They're gorgeous.

There are breath-taking begonias and coleus. I look at their foliage and see unmatched beauty. Others look and say, "How nice. Ho hum." I'll never understand. There are three pots of white justicia, a pot of dancing dolphin vine, and my pride and joy, a strophanthus. I took a chance and ordered it five years ago and it was a successful gamble. Every gardener who sees it is in rictus and even people who don't garden are impressed.

Hanging at regular intervals around the porch are six beautiful, droopy ferns.

When I was a little girl my widowed great-aunts, Iva Ballard McNeece and Corinne Ballard Riley, would spend each warm-weather afternoon sitting idly on the porch. They would be attired in nylon stockings and a cotton dress with a brooch pinned to it. Underneath their beds were dust bunnies, or houth moth, as a young cousin put it. They had their priorities straight. Except for their attire and sitting erect, I'm mostly following suit. More than one person has fallen under the spell of my porch.

Begonias, achimines

Chapter Nine

Henry James said 'summer afternoon' are the most beautiful words in the English language. I disagree. My vote goes to 'I'll pot you up one.'

Over time I fell completely in love with plants and began to collect them voraciously. I don't volunteer, the thought of being a member of anything is anathema to me, and I have a minimal social life. When I'm not gardening, I'm reading. I feel lucky beyond words to have found my passion.

There came a time, September, 2009, when a greenhouse became a necessity for housing my 350 containers, not counting my houseplants. A visitor recently remarked that tending my houseplants could be a full-time job.

I went online and found a greenhouse that suited my purpose. It is 18' x 33' and was made in Denmark, then shipped to Red Wing, Minnesota, then to my house. The builders who erected it made many calls to Red Wing as Denmark's directions differed from directions they were familiar with. When it was finished, they declared it had been a challenge.

The floor is covered with a white weed-block material and tables line three walls. There are eight vents in the roof and a slender iron bar is suspended down the center for hanging plants: three kinds of hoya, a staghorn fern, and a stunning trailing begonia that blooms profusely. Or, as the friend who gave me a start of it said, "It blooms its little heart out." There are two narrow aisles for me to move through to water the plants. Some of the tropicals I've had for many years, one of which is a red-flowered jatropa. I bought a pink-flowered jatropa two years ago. Viva la jatropa!

Below is a list of more, but not all of the potted plants in the greenhouse:

- begonias galore
- bougainvillea, four colors
- cassia arumbosa
- Chinese perfume plant, aglaia odorato
- clerodendrom, Blue Glory Bower ,Cashmere Bouquet, Musical Notes
- clivia, named for Lady Clive, Duchess of Norththumberland
- copper plants, which I lift and over-winter inside because I'm never sure I can find them to buy next year and they are among my favorites.
- cordyline, both red and green, which have grown to a stately size; I love them!
- diplodenia aka mandevilla, red and white. Named after Henry John Mandeville, a minister in Buenos Aires.

- Duranta, I have several of these and they get the same treatment as the copper plants.

- elephant ears

- euphorbia milii, both coral and white, aka crown of thorns. This genus contains 2,000 varieties, including poinsettia. I also have a giant milii that I don't know the correct name for. It wasn't labeled when I spied it, nor was it blooming, but I knew I didn't have one so I bought it. Its blooms are beautiful rose-colored clusters that fade to pale pink. Its thorns are very big.

- ferns

- firebush, hamelia patens

- hibiscus

- justicia, pink, white

- lemon, Meyer

- orchids

- plumbago, blue, white The blue ones have been in the same pots and soil for at least eight years, and they continue to bloom their little hearts out.

- shrimp plants, two colors

- strophanthus

- thunbergia, blue orchid vine

- Weeping Southern yew I rooted this from a cutting taken from the Grand Ole Opry Hotel in Nashville, TN. The head gardener gave me permission and the name.

- aloes, kalanchoes, sedums. There are more, but these are the most important ones and the ones I know the names of.

Greenhouse, September 2009

Inside greenhouse

Chapter Ten

I have a special notebook for my orchid inventory. They are all numbered, the variety named, the date, price, and the place I bought them are recorded. I'm up to number 156 but quite a few have died. I have several reliable bloomers, and there are those that are not. I have a seven-year-old oncidium that was blooming when I bought it but has not bloomed since. The plant is beautifully healthy, continues to grow, but has it bloomed? Never. There are those who would have tossed it long ago but I never will. I'm positive my attention will be rewarded someday. I do regret not taking a picture of it when it was in bloom.

I also keep a journal for all my other plants. They don't have an inventory number but the date, price and place of purchase are recorded along with the name of the plant. In addition to these journals I label a large manilla envelope with the year and put labels and receipts into it in case I have to return a plant. This has stood me in good stead numerous times. Some plants are guaranteed for a year and if they don't live up to their guarantee, back they go for a refund.

Dendrobium aggregatum

Pass-along cymbidium

Sweet Sharry Baby −Very fragrant

Oncidium Wildcat Rainbow

This dendrobium was purchased, blooming, April 2008. It, and a keiki, bloomed again April 2014. The fragrance is wonderful.

**I bought this cattleya in a package February 2012.
It first bloomed in April 2014.**

Nun's Orchid

Chapter Eleven

Now, to the very last area of my yard. It is northeast of my house on the edge of the woods, slopes down to the pond and is dominated by three old oak trees. I call the top part Hell's Half Acre. I've put in lots of plants and they're reluctant to thrive. The soil is difficult to dig unless there's been good rain. I layered it with newspapers and leaf mold, which Chuck E., in his exuberant puppy-ness, scattered all over the yard. He did this as a diversion from chewing my water hoses into small pieces. That was expensive. He is so sweet. He loves me with consummate devotion, as dogs are wont to do, and of discipline he has not one whit. Neither does Coco.

Under the three oak trees near the pond are planted seven varieties of Japanese maples, two rhododendrons, a witch hazel, a snow cypress and a number of white azaleas. Just to prove I'm not exaggerating when I talk about my collection, I'll continue the list.

- althea, double pink
- camellia, white
- azalea GeorgeTabor

- buckeye
- crabapple
- cryptomeria
- cypress, Leland
- hydrangeas, Nikko Blue, oakleaf, peegee
- magnolia, Japanese
- monkey puzzle tree
- redbud
- roses
- spirea, Bridal wreath, Vanhouttei
- strawberry bush, native
- sweet olive

A seven-foot by eighty-foot border of daffodils/narcissus is planted along the edge of the woods.

Other trees planted about the yard are sugar maple, European Mountain ash and a deciduous conifer cypress.

Strophanthus

Achillea and cleome

Begonias surrounding cordyline

Crape myrtle

Clematis

Hibiscus

Mina lobata in snuff bottle

Square Garden

Watercolor by Julie Woolfolk

Vivian with crinum lilies

Confederate rose

February garden

Clerodendrum – musical notes

Alternanthera, coleus, blue torenia

Cassia arumbosa

Firespike – odontonema strictum

Indian Pink

Coleus with purple heart

Arum-Dragon Flower

Carrion Flower-Stapelia Gigertea

Both flowers on this page are pollinated by green flies.

Begonia

Caladiums

Locust Purple Robe

Chapter Twelve

Poison ivy? No problem. I am allergic to it, and here's how I deal with it. I leave a door ajar so I can get into the house without touching it, then I pull the evil stuff up using only one bare hand. I am usually able to get the roots. Then I run inside and wash my hands thoroughly. I must accomplish this in five to eight minutes, no shilly-shallying around. I don't wear gloves because the poison ruins them. For most of my life I believed Virginia Creeper and poison ivy were one and the same. Then I learned the ditty, 'Leaves of three, let it be, leaves of five, let it thrive.' This has freed me up quite a lot.

Chapter Thirteen

I wanted bigger and more bountiful blooms so I ordered a beehive with all the necessary accompaniments. Off I went to the bee-seller. I bought a queen and her attendants in a small cage which I placed, with trepidation, in the back floor of my car. They stayed in the cage, calm as could be, all the way home. I had been instructed to keep a constant supply of sugar water, akin to simple syrup, in the receptacle for it. I bought pound upon pound of sugar. I went away for a few days and had someone come and make sure the solution was always available. I have had two swarms of bees to 1. settle in my chimney, and 2. settle in one of the oak trees. They were not provided with a constant supply of sugar water. It caused me to wonder. My bees died. The house across the road had their Bermuda grass lawn sprayed regularly to kill the weeds and various crops in the vicinity were sprayed for insects. Who knows? My bees were dead. I gave the hive box to a neighbor who has better luck than I with bees. That was nine years ago and I haven't tried it since.

Great-uncle Burr – the pharmacist who married my great-aunt Corinne Ballard and who tried to fatten me up with vitamins – in all innocence, did a dreadful thing. He planted kudzu in the woods behind the house. There was a time, in my salad days when I was green, when I brooded excessively about almost everything. I no longer do that but I fervently hope someone comes up with something selective that will eradicate kudzu.

I attempted to do so with a pair of nanny goats, Blanche and Louise. Nobody encouraged me in this venture, quite the opposite. I bought two very long medium-weight chains and attached one end to the goats and the other end to two cement blocks. I put a block of salt and a bucket of water in the goats' proximity. They were out amongst the kudzu. It took a short time for the dogs to settle down, then all went well. Late one night I heard CLANG, CLANG, CLANG. One of the goats had caught her horns in the bail of the water bucket. Yes, unless the goat man had foisted a billy on me, nanny goats can have horns and a goatee. If I were to get any sleep I had to go into the woods and remove the bail from the goat's horns. Back to things going well, until one Sunday afternoon when I had a dozen or so guests come to admire the perennials in the square garden. We were sitting decoratively under the pecan tree sipping cool drinks when from down the road came a roar: "Get these g--d--- goats out of my cows." Two of the more adventurous gentlemen rose to the occasion with alacrity and honored the neighbor's request. I rang the goat man up and said, "I'm not asking for a refund but will you please come and take your goats back? This is not working out." And so he did and the kudzu grows on.

If, at the end of the day, I'm covered with a goodly amount of terra firma and am bone tired, I count it a successful day in the garden. In the shower the dirt sluices down the drain and I'm energized. If I've thought ahead and I have something nice to eat, I feel like I have the world by the tail. After that, I put on a CD, light a candle, write in my journal and go to bed anticipating a replica of today when I wake up.

My Garden My Homeplace

Afterword

You may be wondering why I wrote this book. Well, the mood just hit me. It's a book that I would enjoy reading, and I hope some of my experience will help other gardeners. If you encounter something that sets your teeth on edge, keep in mind I'm a gardener, not an English Composition teacher. In addition, I strongly believe stories should be told and the past remembered.

Ann Ballard

Made in the USA
Lexington, KY
12 February 2015